Voices of the River

Adventures on the Delaware

by Jan Cheripko

Boyds Mills Press

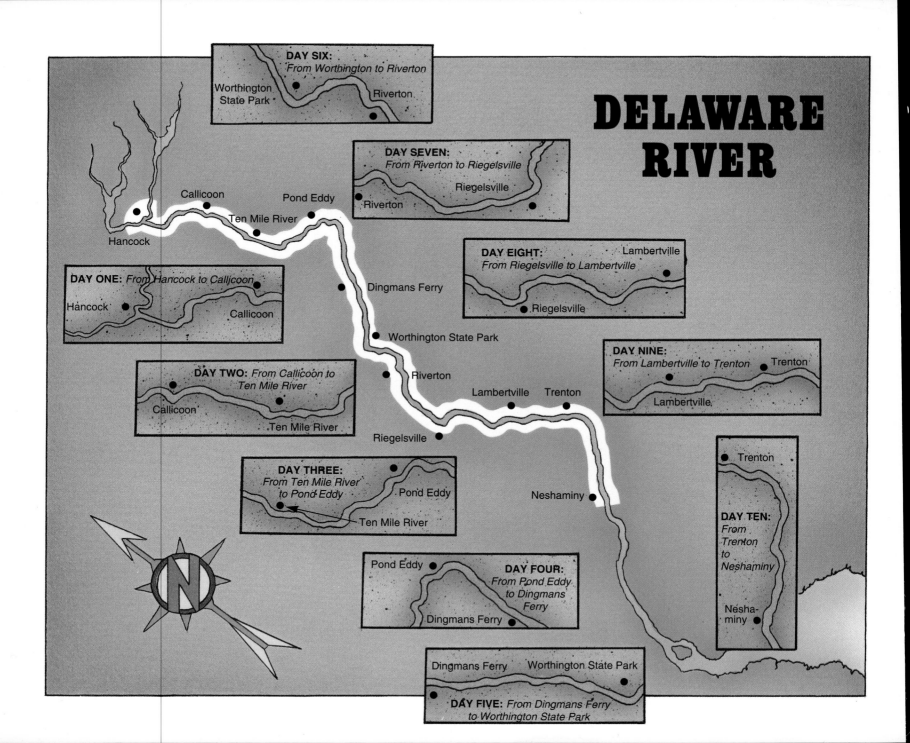

Map **2**

Introduction By Matthew Smith **5**

Chapter 1 Rain, Trout, and an Eagle **7**

Chapter 2 Big Rapids Ahead **11**

Chapter 3 A Famous Author and Then More Rapids **15**

Chapter 4 Into the Middle Delaware **19**

Chapter 5 With the Wind in Your Face **23**

Chapter 6 Through the Water Gap **27**

Chapter 7 Past Foul Rift **29**

Chapter 8 A Day with Kayakers, Then a Surprise **31**

Chapter 9 Rapids at Start and Finish, and a Crossing **37**

Chapter 10 A Tough Ending **41**

Epilogue By Matthew Smith **44**

Addendum You Might Like to Know **45**

Index **48**

To my wife, Valray, and my daughter, Julia

First and foremost, my sincere thanks to Matthew Smith. Not many fourteen-year-old boys have the stamina to do what he did.

Special thanks to Stan Pratt, James Schell, and Ken and Sandy Schultz for their photographic contributions.

Grateful thanks also to Jim and Patty Smith, Bud and Mary Smith, Dr. John and Betty Petkus, Mike Ryan, Carol Frankowicz of the Coast Guard Auxiliary, Arlene Prentiss, Fran O'Hagen and Mike Holt; to John Hutzky, superintendent, Mike Reuber, South District ranger, and other members of the Upper Delaware River National Park Service; to Rick Lander of Lander's River Trips, David Jones of Kittatinny Canoes, and Mike McBrien of Point Pleasant Canoes and Tubes; to William Douglass, executive director of the Upper Delaware Council; to Christopher Roberts of the Delaware River Basin Commission; Jack's Marina; to Mary Curtis; Fred Lewis; Teg Hughes; Paul Mang of Northeast Sports; Nancy Wolfe; Jim Magill; and Gary Letcher, author of *Canoeing the Delaware River;*

To Gregg Birnbaum, John and Debra Conway, and Doug Cunningham and all of my friends at the *Times Herald-Record;*

To Peter Lourie, who gave me the idea;

To my many friends at Boyds Mills Press, especially Dr. Christine San José, my editor; Tim Gillner, my art director; Mary Heaton, Hugh Rechner, Larry Rosler, Jeff O'Hare, Thomas R. White, Leah White, Jan Keen, Joan O'Donnell, and Pamela Sader;

To Kent L. Brown Jr. for helping me figure out a way to do this;

And last, thanks to my family, Peggy Wills, Shari Knapp, and Justin Knapp, and to my wife, Valray, and my daughter, Julia, who patiently waited and worried.

Text copyright © 1993 by Jan Cheripko
Photographs copyright © 1993 by Jan Cheripko, except where otherwise noted in credits
All rights reserved

Published by Caroline House
Boyds Mills Press, Inc.
A Highlights Company
815 Church Street
Honesdale, Pennsylvania 18431
Printed in Mexico

Publisher Cataloging-in-Publication Data
Cheripko, Jan.
  Voices of the river : adventures on the Delaware / by Jan Cheripko.
[48]p. : col. ill. ; cm.
Summary : A photo journal chronicling a 215-mile, ten-day canoe trip from Hancock, New York, down to Philadelphia, Pennsylvania, taken by a fourteen-year-old boy and a forty-year-old writer.
ISBN 1-56397-325-1 (hardcover) ISBN 1-56397-622-6 (paperback)
1. Delaware River (N.Y.-Del. and N.J.)—Description and travel—Juvenile literature. 2. Upper Delaware National Scenic and Recreational River (N.Y. and Pa.)—Juvenile literature. 3. Canoes and canoeing—Delaware River (N.Y.-Del. and N.J.)—Juvenile literature. [1. Delaware River (N.Y.-Del. and N.J.)—Description and travel. 2. Canoes and canoeing—Delaware River (N.Y.-Del. and N.J.).] I. Title.
974.9—dc20   1993   CIP
Library of Congress Catalog Card Number 93-71611

First Boyds Mills Press paperback edition, 1996
Book designed by Tim Gillner
The text of this book is set in 11-point Stone Serif.

10 9 8 7 6 5 4 3 2

Map by Rob Sepanek

Photographs: Charlie Cary: 29 (left); Jan Cheripko: Pages 8, 9, 10, 13, 18, 20, 21, 22, 23, 24, 25, 27, 28 (bottom right), 29, 30, 31, 32, 33, 34, 35, 36, 37, 38, 39, 41, 42, 44, and 45; Stan Pratt: Pages 1, 2, 6, 9, 11, and 12; Jim Schell: Pages 26, 28, and 46 (right); Ken Schultz: Pages 5, 14, 15, 16, 17, 19, and 46 (left); and Patricia Smith: Pages 40, 43, and 44 (top).

INTRODUCTION

My name is Matthew Smith. I'm fourteen years old, and this is the story of a 215-mile canoe trip I took with Jan Cheripko. We traveled from Hancock, New York, where the main part of the Delaware River starts, to Philadelphia, where the river becomes too big for canoes.

Jan is forty-one years old, and he's a friend of my parents. He's a writer. It was his idea to take this trip, and he asked me to come along so that he could show what canoeing the Delaware River was like for a teenager.

At first, I wasn't sure I wanted to go. I didn't want to spend my whole summer canoeing and miss basketball camp.

It turned out that the trip could be done in ten days, if everything went right. I could still go to basketball camp. I think my father helped convince me to go on the trip. He told me that he wished he'd had a chance to do something like this when he was a kid. He told me that I would remember this trip for the rest of my life.

I'm not an expert canoeist, and neither is Jan. Each of us has canoed only about four or five times. But I think anybody can take a trip like this. You have to do some planning, like where you're going to stay and what you'll eat. And you have to be smart about the river. You have to scout the rapids to see what they're like.

My father told me that the river would teach me something. He was right.

I learned that there are a lot of things to do out there, a lot of possibilities in life. It's just a matter of choosing one and doing it.

I learned about frustration—the way to get past it is to keep on doing whatever you're doing. No matter what it is, keep doing it. Then you get good at it.

And I learned about the river. I learned how to read rapids and follow the river's current. I learned how to hide from head winds in coves and behind clumps of trees when you're going through long eddies.

I learned to love the sight of the white underside of leaves when the wind is at your back. And to hate the sight when the wind is in your face.

I don't know if I'm a different person after this trip or not. I think maybe I am, but I don't know exactly how or why.

But I learned something important about myself—I am not a good beginner, but once I start something, I'll see it through to the end.

One last thing. When you spend ten days with someone, ten days paddling a canoe for eight to ten hours a day, you don't always get along. And that's okay.

Matthew Smith

CHAPTER 1 — Rain, Trout, and an Eagle –
From Hancock to Callicoon

A wet, soggy mist hung over the river. Gray and black clouds floated above us as Matthew and I carried our seventeen-foot Grumman aluminum canoe down to the Delaware at the tip of Point Mountain near Hancock. Like the fog-draped world around us, we were wrapped in hazy dreams. We weren't thinking that this was the first day of a long, long journey. Or if we thought about it at all, we didn't know how far 215 miles really is, or how long ten days on the river will last.

I thought to myself, "Oh well, we're going canoeing. We'll have a nice time."

Starting something you've never done before isn't easy. You feel a lot of confusion. Your body rushes forward with excitement ready to get going, but your mind holds you back with its warnings that hard work and danger lie ahead.

Having people around helps you get started, at least that's the way Matthew and I felt. It would have been hard to say, "I've changed my mind. I don't want to go." But we both certainly thought about not going, right up until we shoved off.

It was July 5, 1992. We planned to pull our canoe out of the river ten days later at Neshaminy State Park, a few miles north of Philadelphia.

But this was day one of our trip. With Point Mountain watching over us we walked across the grassy field, past clumps of small riverbank trees, and down the dirt path dropping sharply towards the river. Ahead of us the Delaware roiled and gurgled.

At the point where its East and West branches slide into one another, the Delaware River is about a football field wide from bank to bank. It's filled with a smattering of rapids, deep pools, and dark channels. This morning, after days of on-and-off rain, the Delaware ran fast and strong at the start of its long journey to the Atlantic Ocean.

Matt's father, Jim, had helped us paint "Hancock to Philadelphia" on the side of our boat. We had fastened plastic seats with back supports to the canoe's metal seats. Next to sunscreen lotion and paddles, those seats were the most important things we had.

We had bought lightweight, basswood, bent-shaft paddles. They weren't cheap, but they were worth it. We brought along extra aluminum paddles so that we wouldn't break the wooden ones on the big rocks in the rapids. We didn't have much gear with us, because for the first few nights we would stay either at my house or Matt's house. Since we were not experienced canoeists, we figured it would be smart not to take camping equipment through the rapids where there was a good chance of tipping over. Further downriver, we would load in the camping gear.

I sat in the back, because I thought it would be easier to take photos that way. I also figured that Matt had better eyesight than I had and could see the rapids and rocks better.

A photographer snapped pictures of us as we pushed our canoe into the water at the exact spot

Dark clouds hang over us, and ahead lie 215 miles of the Delaware River.

Matt's second rainbow trout from the Delaware—an eighteen-inch beauty.

where the East and West branches of the Delaware River meet.

We were off.

Less than an hour later the low, white clouds started to spray a soft drizzle into our faces. Soon, the clouds were black and heavy and pelting us with cold, hard rain. We paddled on silently, and though we didn't say it then, we both were thinking what a stupid idea canoeing the Delaware was.

"Might as well fish," Matt mumbled.

He pulled out a silver Rapala, hooked it onto his fishing line, and threw it toward a pool as we floated through a small rapid. A Rapala is a long, shiny lure that is supposed to look like a minnow to a trout. Matt's father and grandfather taught him to fish, and he's pretty good at it.

The Delaware River is full of fish, especially native trout that love the cold waters of the Upper Delaware. They're not easy to catch.

Suddenly Matt got a yank on his lure. A few minutes later, he landed a small rainbow trout—his first from the Delaware. It wasn't large enough to keep. Matt's grandfather told him it's best to release most of the trout you catch so there will always be enough in the river.

We maneuvered past a small island and then through another riffle, where we got hung up on a rock. That would happen a lot in the early part of the trip. We hopped out into the cold water to pull the canoe off the rock.

Even though we were wearing waterproof parkas, we were both already soaked from the rain, so we didn't bother to roll up our sweat pants. We both wore rubber-soled river shoes that keep you from slipping on the slick rocks in the river.

Matt studied a deep, black pool nearby. I stood waist deep in the little riffle and watched as he tossed his lure into it. After a ten-minute struggle, Matt hauled in an eighteen-inch rainbow.

"I had a feeling that would be a good spot for trout," Matt said. "I can't tell you what it feels like to catch such a beautiful fish," he said after he let the fish go. "I was afraid I would lose it. That always goes through your mind. Whenever you catch a big fish, you think, 'I'm never going to catch a big one.' But sometimes you do."

The first day would be our longest—26.5 miles from the start of the main river to Callicoon.

By the time we hit Lordville, New York, nine miles south of Hancock, the sun finally came out.

We saw few people, just a scatter of fishermen at the little village of Equinunk, Pennsylvania. And we saw great blue herons and wild ducks. We lost count, but we figure we saw more than fifty great blue herons and more than one thousand wild ducks by the end of our trip.

When we pulled into Long Eddy about fifteen miles from Hancock, six from Lordville, for a short break, the sun had disappeared. Big, black clouds were rolling in behind us. We could hear the rumble of thunder chasing us, and we kept watching for lightning. Two guys in an aluminum canoe in the middle of a wide eddy would be sitting ducks for lightning.

An eddy is a long, wide stretch of a river, almost like a lake. You never get a true sense of the whole Delaware River, because the river winds through mountains. And often the mountains reach down to the edge of the river, blocking out your view of the river you just came through. It's more like canoeing from one lake, or eddy, to another. You come out of an eddy, through a set of rapids, and into another eddy. And when you finish that eddy and look behind you, you don't see the last eddy. All you see are mountains.

We also found out why Long Eddy got its name. Long Eddy is a very long eddy, especially when the wind is shooting tiny bullets of rain into your face.

When we pushed off again, the clouds were right overhead and it was pouring. That's when we made a big mistake. We went to the left of a large island and found ourselves hung up on a long gravel bar. We ended up dragging our canoe over the rocks and gravel for more than one hundred yards.

The river shoes kept us from slipping, but our ankles were scraped and bruised and our backs were plenty sore.

A couple of miles south of Long Eddy we came across nine mute swans that had made the Delaware River home. We knew about these big white birds. Two

We see few people the first day, only a fisherman here and there wrapped in the river's ancient majesty and mystery.

of them used to live on a pond nearby. A couple of years ago they wandered over to the river. Now there are several of them. Mute swans aren't really afraid of humans. If you get too close, they'll spread their wings and hiss. If they have young nearby, they'll even come after you. Some of the fishermen don't like them for that. But they are very beautiful.

The clouds moved slowly away from us, heading east to our left, as we glided slowly past the swans. Behind us, an occasional car rumbled across the highway bridge over Basket Brook. Here, the road comes close to the river, but there are stretches in the Upper Delaware where cars and houses and people are far removed. We paddled through several such places on this first day. There, the air settles in around you and all you hear are the rhythmic strokes of your paddle slipping through the dark water.

From a distance, the Delaware looks one dirty-brown color. But when you're sliding along on top of it, you discover it's really dozens of different colors and shades.

In places, the river is so clear you can see eight feet down or more. But moments later it's deep, dark, and lovely, daring you to dive into its jet black waters to discover the answer to some ancient mystery.

Next, you're slipping through a pea-green channel past the gnarled and tangled roots of hemlock trees straining to hold on to what's left of moss-covered river banks.

Or you might pull up toward a flat stretch of field where the wild rye grass will hide you all day, and when you step into the sun-drenched copper shallows, the bathwater river massages your aching feet and sunburnt legs.

An eagle leaves its dining spot on a tree branch.

Ahead, the sparkle of thousands of miniature stars dancing on the tips of tiny waves calls you forward and soon you're crashing into the wild and power of another rushing rapid.

Dark mysteries, sun-drenched shallows, crashing rapids—the Delaware is all that and much more.

Around 4 p.m. we neared Hankins, twenty miles from Hancock, and hit our first surprise on the river.

We had maps of the entire Delaware, from Hancock to Trenton, that showed where the current was and where the rapids were. The rapids are graded, from Class I to Class VI. One is the easiest, six the hardest. These maps were put out by the Delaware River Basin Commission, and generally, they're pretty good. But the ones we had were from 1979, and a river can change a lot in thirteen years. (Newer maps, updated in 1991, are now available.)

We found islands that weren't noted on the maps, and eel weirs (traps) that didn't appear, and we also thought that some of the rapids, like the ones in Hankins, were not correctly marked.

Maybe it was the high water from the rain, or simply that we weren't expecting big waves, but the Class I Plus rapid near Hankins bounced us around more than we expected. The river narrowed to a fast channel to our right as we headed into the rapid. There wasn't much room to avoid it.

Rapids are sneaky. You come up on them faster than you realize, and before you know it, you're in them. That's what happened to us. We plowed into the waves expecting them to be about a foot and a half high, and then all of sudden, the waves were two and a half feet high, and we were getting soaked.

"That was more than a Class I Plus," Matt yelled to me as we skipped through the last waves thirty yards later.

A couple of miles north of Callicoon, the sun broke through the late afternoon haze. Right overhead, just to our left, an eagle flew by! It circled back toward us and less than thirty yards away dived into the water and came up with a fish. Then it flew to a nearby tree and settled down for dinner.

We hadn't expected to see eagles until we got farther south. Seeing it here was Mother Nature's reward for sticking with our trip. Day one ended on a high.

It was 7 p.m. when we pulled the canoe ashore and hid it in some tall weeds underneath the Callicoon Bridge. We had been on the river for more than ten hours. We were exhausted. My wife, Valray, met us and drove us to our house in Hankins where Matthew and I would spend the first night. Tomorrow we faced Skinners Falls, our first Class II rapid.

CHAPTER 2   Big Rapids Ahead –
Callicoon to Ten Mile River

We shoot through Skinners Falls, the first big rapid of the trip.

If we were up to it, we would reach Lackawaxen, twenty-four miles downriver, today. If not, we would stop at Ten Mile River, seventeen miles from Callicoon.

We had to go through our first Class II rapid, Skinners Falls, considered by many as one of the most difficult on the river. The falls are named for Daniel Skinner, called the Admiral of the Delaware because he was the first to float rafts down to Trenton and Philadelphia in the early 1700s.

By the 1800s, rafting was a big industry along the Upper Delaware. It was often a family business, with women and children taking the trip as well. At its peak, more than three thousand rafts a year were floated downstream to Trenton and Philadelphia. One man, Deacon Mitchell, once floated a raft from Callicoon to Trenton, about two hundred miles, in two and a half days. The logs from the rafts were used for masts on sailing ships and for houses.

Once the rafters unloaded their logs, they would walk back home or, after the canals were built in the

Yesterday's rain had blown over. This morning, the sky was deep blue and filled with white, puffy clouds floating above us. Matt took his shirt off, but I left mine on. Even though it rained most of yesterday, I already had some sunburn on the tops of my feet. You can really get burnt sitting in an aluminum canoe all day long. We greased ourselves with sunscreen lotion and headed downriver.

Skinners Falls is not only popular with boaters and swimmers, but sun-bathers like it as well.

early 1800s, they might hitch a ride on a boat being towed upriver by mules.

Rafting was a very dangerous business. The rafters usually waited until the high water of spring floods when the current was the strongest to maneuver their 125-foot-long and 25-foot-wide pine and hemlock rafts past the rocks and through rapids. Many of the rafters were killed.

Today, people still drown in the Delaware River every year. It's not high water from spring floods that kills them. Instead, the canoeists, rafters, or swimmers who die often don't know the river well. Many are drunk or high on drugs, and usually they're not wearing life jackets.

For canoeists, most of the rapids on the Delaware are not too dangerous, but some, like Skinners Falls, need to be scouted ahead of time. A week before our trip, Matt and I had studied how to go through these rapids.

We discovered that there was one chute in the middle of the big rocks that would be the best way through the falls. Now, as we approached the falls, we pulled the canoe into a little backwater eddy among the big rocks.

A friend, Stan Pratt, had been taking photos of us yesterday and today. We waited for him to climb onto one of the big rocks so that he could get a good photo of us going through the rapids. Most of the other people going ahead of us got hung up on the rocks.

We pulled our canoe into the main river and lined it up with the chute we wanted to hit. Once we got into the current, there wasn't much to do but keep paddling. We shot through with no trouble. One rapid down, eight big ones to go.

You get a strange feeling when you approach a rapid. You're sort of nervous but excited, too. You know you're going to go through with it and not chicken out. And even with Class II rapids, which can have big waves and lots of rocks, you don't think you're going to get hurt. Still, there's this uneasy feeling of not knowing what to expect.

Then you shoot into the rapid. A tremendous surge of speed and power overwhelms you. You battle to keep control while

We had scouted Skinners Falls, picked our route, and hit the chute perfectly.

the river pulls you forward and bounces you around. And everywhere there's water. It's beating you in your face. It's spilling all over you into the boat. And sometimes, in a big rapid, there are a few seconds that last like a day, where you think, "Oh no! We're not going to make it."

But we did make it this time. We went through our first Class II rapid without tipping over.

From there it was on to Narrowsburg, a spot where the banks on the New York and Pennsylvania sides come close together, and the water is dark black and 113 feet deep.

We pulled up to the public access and sat on the grass eating a picnic lunch with Matt's parents, Jim and Patty, his brothers, Peter, David, and James Patrick, and some of his other relatives, along with Valray and my daughter, Julia.

We stretched out our cramped legs and lay in the thick green grass looking up at the puffy white clouds floating through the deep blue sky.

A couple of miles south of Narrowsburg we went under an old train trestle, built around 1851, when the Great New York and Erie Railway from Hoboken, New Jersey, to Dunkirk, New York, was completed. We had gone under several car bridges, but this was the only train trestle on the Upper Delaware. Today, the trains carry freight, not people. Some people along the river worry that the freight trains could derail and spill toxic chemicals into the river. Bed and breakfast owners and merchants would like to see the trains carry people again, just as in the 1800s.

By the end of this second day, our backs, upper arms, and butts were pretty sore. But we had made it through Skinners Falls without capsizing.

For the next few nights until we got into the Middle Delaware, we would stay at Matt's house nearby in Yulan, New York. Tomorrow we faced more big rapids.

Freight trains still rumble up and down the tracks along the Delaware. Long ago, they carried settlers heading west and then vacationers from the cities.

At Narrowsburg, where the banks of the Delaware come close together, the river is 113 feet deep.

Thirty vultures sat in a big sycamore tree across the river from where we put in our canoe to start the third day. That didn't seem like a good sign.

Matt's father and his two brothers, David and Peter, were going to join us today. Two of my friends, Ken Schultz and Sandy Speers, came along, too. We would be a flotilla of three canoes.

Ken writes for *Field & Stream* magazine. He's also written and photographed several books about fishing. He took some of the photos in this book. Sandy works for the National Park Service. She took the day off so that she could paddle the canoe while Ken took pictures. Ken and Sandy got married shortly after this trip.

Today would test our paddling skills. We would go through four Class II or Class II Minus rapids and several Class I Plus rapids.

The first rapid we hit was Colang Rift, where Colang Creek flows into the Delaware from Pennsylvania.

Ken was downriver on a big rock, ready to take pictures when we went through the rapid, but we got hung up on a rock upriver. Matt figured it was my fault that we got stuck. He thought I wasn't paddling on the right side at the right time. I thought he should have been telling me where the rocks were, since he would see them before I did. At any rate, we must have looked pretty silly struggling to get off the rock. Ken didn't like the pictures he got, so we had to pull the canoe back upstream through the rapid and do it all over again.

This time we did fine. We still hadn't swamped.

At Colang Rift, Matt takes a break from a long day of paddling to horse-play with his brothers.

A few miles south we went through Narrows Falls Rift, this time with no trouble. So far we had been pretty lucky. We hadn't even taken in much water and didn't need to bail.

The next stop was Lackawaxen, Pennsylvania, the home of author Zane Grey. Zane Grey is considered the master of the western novel. He wrote more than one hundred books. His most famous is *Riders of the Purple Sage*. Today, Zane Grey's house is a museum. We visited there for a short while and then headed south underneath the Roebling Bridge, the oldest suspension bridge in the United States, built by John Augustus Roebling, who would go on to build the Brooklyn Bridge.

Smooth as a mirror, the Delaware reflects the cirrus clouds—Mare's Tails, the farmers call them—drifting through the blue sky twenty thousand feet or more above us.

Matt and I speak with Park Ranger Don Sledz at the Zane Grey Museum in Lackawaxen. Matt's grandfather, Bud, and grandmother, Mary, tour the museum with us.

It is also at Lackawaxen that Chief Joseph Brandt, the son of an English lord and a native American woman, defeated a local militia that tried to surprise his army as they crossed the Delaware. Brandt fought for the English during the Revolution.

On that fateful day, one of the American soldiers mistakenly shot his musket, warning Brandt. The mistake was costly for the colonists. Outnumbered and outarmed, only a few of the revolutionaries escaped.

Just beyond Roebling Bridge we maneuvered past an eel trap and almost tipped over in the rapids. Eel weirs, or eel traps, can be a problem for canoeists. Sometimes they can even be dangerous, especially when they aren't marked.

People have been trapping eels on the Delaware for more than one hundred years. Once they catch them, they "smoke" the eels—cook them inside small huts for a long time over wood coals—and sell them to fish markets, mostly in New York City, where they're considered a delicacy.

We saw a lot of eels. At first, they're kind of ugly, but the more you watch them you realize how beautiful and fascinating they are. They grow to about two or three feet long. Every autumn the adult eels leave freshwater rivers like the Delaware and swim hundreds of miles to the Sargasso Sea in the Atlantic Ocean to spawn. The adults never come back, but their offspring do.

The traps built to catch eels are made of two rows of stones meeting in a V. For canoeists, the best thing to do is to go around an eel weir, but you can't always see them. Once you're inside the V, you have to paddle towards one of the rock walls and pull your canoe over it. If you go through the trap at the end of the V, you might get hung up.

The trap at the end of the eel weir is made up of wooden slats built so that an eel falls through them into a large container but can't get out. If your canoe gets hung up in the trap, you must get out to pull the canoe through. And you have to avoid stepping on a nail or getting your foot trapped in the wooden slats.

We still had two more Class II rapids—Big Cedar Rift and Shohola Rift—to go today.

Ken and Sandy went through the three-foot waves of Big Cedar first. Sandy is a very experienced canoeist who knows the Upper Delaware well, so we watched closely. We followed their route with no problems.

Matt's father and his brothers left us after Big Cedar.

At Shohola Rift, which is a Class II rapid followed closely by a Class I Plus and two Class I rapids, we ran into trouble. We went safely through the Class II, but then we got badly hung up. The back of the canoe spun around and smashed into a rock, almost throwing Matt overboard. Now we were sitting sideways in the rapid, and we were almost taking in water. If that happened we would swamp.

Angrily, Matt slammed his hand against the side of the canoe.

"My lure broke!" Matt fumed. "My silver Rapala! When we hit the rock!"

"We can worry about that later," I snapped. "First, let's get off this rock."

By shifting our weight, rocking, and pushing off with our strong aluminum paddles, we freed the canoe, but we went through the rapids backwards.

Silently we floated into a small eddy.

I knew Matt was mad because we kept getting hung up on rocks. I knew he thought it was my fault for not steering the canoe right. But I was having a hard time seeing the rocks.

It was there that Matt and I had our first argument.

"Listen, do you want to go on with this trip or not?" I demanded.

"Yeah," he answered quietly.

"Okay, but things aren't going to always go the way they should. I'm going to do some things wrong, and you're going to do some things wrong. We can't afford to stay mad at each other.

"And we have to figure out a way so that we don't get hung up on rocks. I'll start wearing my glasses so that I can see better. But you'll see the rocks before I do. You just tell me which side to paddle on, and that's the side I'll paddle on. We've got to learn to trust each other if we're going to do this trip."

We kept to our agreement, and our system worked. By the end of the day, Matt didn't even have to say which side to paddle on. As soon as he switched sides I switched sides. For the most part that worked, although sometimes, when we would come right up to a chute through rocks, I would switch to get the back of the canoe through the chute without hitting the rocks.

A few miles later we met up with Ken and Sandy. Ken took some more photos, and then we said good-bye.

By late afternoon, heavy white clouds began to cover the afternoon sun. Through the thin haze rising from the river we watched a deer wander down a bank to get a drink of water.

We pulled out of the river about 6:30 at Paul Kean's landing at Pond Eddy. Paul is a friend of Matt's father, and he let us store our canoe there overnight.

"Be careful tomorrow," Paul told us. "There's a dangerous eel weir just up ahead, and it's not clearly marked."

Looking for an unmarked eel weir tomorrow morning when the river would be covered in fog wasn't going to be fun.

With the Roebling Bridge in the background, we head into another small rapid.

CHAPTER 4 〰 Into the Middle Delaware –
From Pond Eddy to Dingmans Ferry

Just as we figured, the river was blanketed in thick, silvery-white fog. By midmorning most of the fog would burn away, but as we pushed off it was heavy enough to keep us from seeing the eel weir that Paul Kean had told us about.

The trap was built on a narrow bend, and it stretched almost completely across the river, so there wasn't much room to get around it. We were actually inside the V when we realized what was going on. We back-paddled and pulled the canoe around to the right of the trap on the Pennsylvania side of the river. As we scooted around the edge of the eel trap, we had a few choice adjectives to describe the trap's builder.

We still had six Class I Plus rapids and one Class II Minus rapid ahead of us. We hadn't tipped over yet, but we knew that we had to face Mongaup Falls, where the Mongaup River flows into the Delaware, and it had some big waves and tricky currents.

We were getting pretty good at not hitting rocks, and while we didn't talk about it, I knew we both hoped to finish the trip without capsizing. There are some dangerous rapids in the Lower Delaware as well, but there aren't too many of them. We knew if we got past this day, we'd have a real good shot at finishing the trip without tipping over.

In those moments of battling a rapid you find yourself totally concentrating on making it through. Nothing else matters. You're elevated into a sense of yourself, a sense of freedom that most of us today

There's always a rush of excitement when you head into a rapid.

rarely experience. It is a sense of being that the Lenni Lenape who traveled these waters centuries ago probably knew and revered.

In those moments we too knew the freedom.

We made it through Mongaup Falls. And through Stairway Rift before it and through Butlers Falls.

And now we entered the tunnel-like magic beneath the steep, dark cliffs of Hawk's Nest where the sun doesn't reach all morning.

Isolated, pristine, and pure, the Middle Delaware holds plenty of places to spend a hot afternoon.

At Hawk's Nest, the river snakes its way beneath a steep wall of rock.

When we were planning our trip, Matt, his father, and Val, Julia, and I ate breakfast at the Hawk's Nest Restaurant. As we gobbled up our bacon and eggs, we stared at the canoeists hundreds of feet below. Back then, they were only small spots on the river. We knew they were canoes, but we couldn't see the people in them. They were just little silver slivers that floated into view as they came around the bend, slipping away beneath the tree-covered ledges below us and emerging on the other side of the tunnel on their trip downriver.

Now we were the ones going through the tunnel beneath the Hawk's Nest Restaurant. I wondered if anyone was watching us. I looked at a house balanced on the face of the cliff and wondered how anyone could have built it.

I studied the huge blocks of black and gray rock connected like Legos on the side of the mountain by master stonemasons decades earlier when they carved Route 97 out of the mountainside.

I didn't often think about the Lenni Lenape who had lived along the Delaware for centuries before the Europeans came, but I did when I went through Hawk's Nest. It is so peaceful and still. It forces you to remember how old the Earth is, and how ancient some of its people.

By the time we came out from the darkness of Hawk's Nest, we had gone through the last of the rapids of the Upper Delaware. Still we hadn't tipped over. Now we coasted by the small city of Port Jervis, New York.

A fisherman hunts for bait fish near the City of Port Jervis. The high tower in the distance is High Point, New Jersey.

Matt explores the underworld of the river.

A few miles south of Port Jervis, we stopped near where the Neversink River enters the Delaware. Matt stood on the concrete monument that marks the exact spot where New Jersey, New York, and Pennsylvania meet. He fished for 40-pound tiger muskellunge, a deep-water cross between a pike and pure muskie, dreaming that he would catch one. He saw one—maybe. I know we both saw some huge fish come out of the water. They might have been carp, though, because muskies stay down.

By the time we ended the fourth day—we were about halfway through the trip—the sun had faded, and a drizzle began to fall. Just a few minutes after we pulled our canoe out at Dingmans Ferry (established by Andrew Dingman in the early 1700s), two guys in separate canoes pulled up.

It turned out that these guys, Mike Christenberry and James Karcher, knew a lot about the river, especially the part that was still ahead of us. They used to run a camp and often took kids on overnight canoe trips on the Delaware. They had been canoeing on the Delaware more than fifty times, once even at night.

Today, they both took off work just to go canoeing. They told us about the river south of us, and warned us in particular about the wing dams, and about Foul Rift, a dangerous rapid near Belvidere, New Jersey. Mike told us it would be best to portage—walk around—Foul Rift.

Matt and I knew about the Upper Delaware. We knew very little about the Middle Delaware and even less about the lower section. It was good that the rain was now coming down hard, because high water (as long as it wasn't too high) meant a faster current and less chance of hitting rocks in the unknown rapids ahead.

That night, we listened to the pouring rain at Matt's house, glad we weren't camping. Tomorrow night, we would be.

At the end of day four we meet Mike Christenberry, left, and James Karcher, who warn us about Foul Rift on the Lower Delaware.

CHAPTER 5 — With the Wind in Your Face –
Dingmans Ferry to Worthington State Park

We pulled out into the main channel, some thirty yards from shore. An extended stretch of straight river lay ahead, and I knew we were in for a long day: the wind blew steady and strong into our faces.

This is when you learn about frustration. You just keep going straight ahead, because there's nothing else to do. And a curious thing happens. After a while, it's as if you're not even paddling, you're watching someone else paddle. Both Matt and I had the same experience.

You're not tired. Your muscles don't hurt. You just keep paddling. You lose track of time, and you stopped counting strokes a long time ago. You just keep paddling.

You think about things—about home, but you don't feel sad; about food, but you don't eat; about sleep, but you're wide awake. And you just keep paddling.

It's a dream world where time has no meaning. You're just kind of there, on the river. But at the same time, you're not really there, you're watching.

"Sometimes when I'm shooting baskets I've had the same feeling," said Matt. "It's like I see myself shooting, and I know I can't miss."

"Yeah," I agreed. "When I was a kid, playing linebacker in football, I remember playing a game where I knew exactly what the offense was going to do. It was like I was looking down on myself playing this game, and nobody could stop me from making the tackle."

Day five begins with a stiff wind blowing in our faces.

And then in the middle of this day-long fight against the wind, we swung into Wallpack Bend, where the river wraps around and heads in the other direction.

There were no people, no houses, no sound of cars, nothing but the river—and the herons, and the geese, and the ducks. Then suddenly you look at the leaves of the trees and you see that the wind is blowing

The river almost wraps around itself and heads in another direction at Wallpack Bend.

Matt finds time to cool off with snorkeling near Wallpack Bend.

about 70,000 acres, is owned by the National Park Service and the states of Pennsylvania and New Jersey. That night we camped at one of New Jersey's parks—Worthington State Forest, a 5,830-acre park in the Kittatinny Mountains. We pitched our small tent in one of the cleared areas near a section of Old Mine Road, some say the oldest road in the United States. The Appalachian Trail, a 2,015-mile footpath from Georgia to Maine, also runs through Worthington State Forest.

Worthington State Park isn't far from Tocks Island, a place where government officials once planned to dam the Delaware.

The Delaware River is the last major river east of the Mississippi that does not have a dam on its main stem. There are three small wing dams on the river, but they don't stop the water from flowing.

The Tocks Island dam was supposed to be 160 feet high. It would have flooded the whole area that we

Shawnee Resort Hotel is one of the most well known tourist attractions in the Delaware Water Gap.

the other way; that the wind is now at your back. And you sit back and let the wind and the current move you faster than all your paddling all day long could take you. And for that short time all the world seems perfect.

We were in the Middle Delaware now—named by the government, the Delaware Water Gap National Recreation Area. It is at the end of this stretch that the river cuts through the last of the Appalachian Mountains. Like a gaping hole in a huge, tree-covered earth dam, the water gap marks the last bastion of rugged mountain country. Beyond it lie the river towns and large cities carved out of the wilderness by the pioneers of colonial America.

Much of the 40-mile-long Middle Delaware,

had just that day paddled through. The huge reservoir that would have been created would have stretched north for 37 miles to Port Jervis, creating a 250-billion-gallon lake. That's bigger than the two reservoirs on the East and West branches combined.

Supporters of the dam said that the reservoir would control floods in the area, provide water in times of drought, and offer hydropower for electricity.

Opponents argued that the reservoir would wipe out forever one of America's most wild and scenic rivers, would eliminate thousands of homes and businesses, and would cost too much to build.

It now looks as if the Tocks Island dam will not be built. The federal government "de-authorized" the Tocks Island project in 1992. But if the demand for water in the Northeast gets too great, some solution will have to be found. Damming the Delaware is one possibility. Our nation's war between the very real need for more water and the equally important desire to preserve our natural resources will be bitterly fought in the twenty-first century. The Delaware River may be a key battleground.

But at the end of day five, politics was far from our minds. The warmth of a deep-orange sun covered us as Matt cast his lure into the Delaware's brown waters. Behind us, the night's early white moon snuck up in the cool eastern sky.

As I returned from a walk to the camp pay phones, I could hear Matt hollering from the river shore.

"Jan! Jan!" he called.

I ran through the woods, fought my way through the tree branches, and stepped onto the edge of the river bank.

"You should have seen it!" Matt yelled to me. "A big striped bass. I had him. You should have got a picture of that!"

A long, hard day comes to a close for us as Matt fishes for bass from the banks of the New Jersey shoreline.

Worthington State Park, where the Appalachian Trail cuts through, is home for us at the end of day five.

city, and we went underneath a busy bridge, Interstate Route 80. We were seeing more people now.

"Traveling upriver from the water gap would be like going back in time," Matt said. "In the Middle Delaware there's no people, no cars, not even very many houses. Everything is slower."

We went past our first big power plant, the Metropolitan Edison Electric Generating Plant near Portland, Pennsylvania. Two big smokestacks stuck out of the shoreline. A large sign told us to stay away from where they took in water for the plant. We did.

We were past the halfway point of the trip, and I knew now that we were going to make it.

Today, we would actually wind our way through the spectacular Delaware Water Gap. After that lay the flat coastal plain of the Eastern seaboard.

The New Jersey side of the water gap is a sheer cliff, more than 1,500 feet high. We saw a little speck of white way up at the top, climbing.

We were near East Stroudsburg, another large

Today was easy—only nineteen miles. Around 5 p.m. we pulled the canoe ashore in Riverton, Pennsylvania, a tiny village across the river from Belvidere, New Jersey. We walked up the bank to the Hurryback River House, a family homestead built in the 1700s that had been turned into a bed and breakfast, where we would spend the night.

Inns were once very popular along the Delaware. First with rafting, and then in the 1800s with

For eons the river has cut its way through the Delaware Water Gap.

The thousands of streams that feed the Delaware hold treasures all their own, like this little waterfall near the Delaware Water Gap.

the Delaware Canal in Pennsylvania and the Delaware and Raritan Canal in New Jersey, and later the railroad, innkeepers could make a living.

As more and more people used cars, motels along highways became more popular. In recent years, however, many people have rediscovered the beauty of the Delaware, and inns have revived.

Jerry and Arlene Prentiss opened the Hurryback Inn seven years ago. Arlene, whose license plate reads My River, traces her ancestors back to some of the earliest settlers along the Delaware. Today, she battles to keep it from becoming polluted. Some people think she's a fanatic; others think she's dead right.

"It's just too beautiful to lose," Arlene told me. "The only way to save it is to fight and fight."

We showered at the Hurryback River House and then walked across the river to Belvidere, New Jersey, to buy a flashlight, which I had forgotten to bring, and some food for the days ahead. We ate dinner at a Chinese restaurant and talked about whether we would go through the rapids of Foul Rift tomorrow or whether we'd walk around them.

On the way back from Belvidere, we met Teg Hughes, a police officer with the Delaware River Joint Toll Bridge Commission. He told us how to go through Foul Rift.

We had already heard plenty of stories about Foul Rift. I had a book (*Canoeing the Delaware River* by Gary Letcher) that said that Foul Rift was one of the most dangerous rapids on the river.

The river dropped twenty-two feet in a half-mile stretch. There were lots of big rocks, some hidden in the water, and plenty of big waves.

It was Teg who convinced us that we could make it. He drew us a map of how to go through. He said he had canoed in the Upper Delaware and told us that if we had gone through Skinners Falls and all of the other rapids without capsizing, then we could manage Foul Rift. Teg gave us the confidence to at least try.

And tomorrow we would.

Matt finds a nice resting place in the Prentiss backyard on the banks of the Delaware.

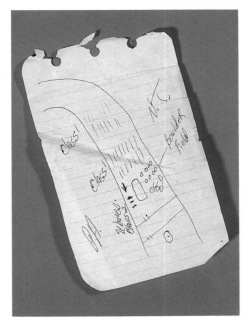

This sketch by Teg Hughes shows the way through Foul Rift.

Teg's drawing matches the reality.

We had heard a lot of stories about Foul Rift, most of them gruesome. "I've seen aluminum canoes wrapped right around those rocks," one man told us.

Matt and I were both nervous, but with our confidence buttressed by Teg Hughes, we were sure we would make it.

Foul Rift is tricky. First, you go through two Class I rapids, and that confuses a lot of people, because they think it's over. They're sitting there thinking, "Oh, that was easy," and then all of a sudden, they're into the two Class II Rapids that really are Foul Rift.

I have a feeling, from talking with other people later on in our trip, that we had high water for these rapids. That made it easier. Maybe it was just that we had gotten so much experience on so many other rapids upriver. Whatever the reason, Foul Rift wasn't as bad as we had expected

We did exactly as Teg had told us. You can see what he said by looking at the map he drew. We came through the two Class I rapids and then stayed to the right, on the Pennsylvania side of the river. The New Jersey side is just a wall of huge boulders. Then we looked for the middle chute through the next ridge of rocks. Finally we angled back to the right to find the chute through the last ridge of rocks.

Then we sat back and let the strong current coming out of the rapid carry us. And for the first time, we had to bail water we had taken in from big waves.

A couple of miles later we went through Capush Rift, which is two Class I Plus rapids. The high water helped us through Foul Rift, but it made some of the

Easton, Pennsylvania, where the Lehigh River meets the Delaware, is the first really large city you hit coming south on the river.

waves in the Class I Plus rapids higher than we expected. Capush Rift was a lot of fun, though. The waves were big, but they covered the rocks so we could glide right over without getting hung up. We took in water and had to bail some more.

About ten miles later we were floating by the stately old homes that line the steep riverbanks in the city of Easton, Pennsylvania. A few people walking along the grassy avenue on top of the bank stopped to study us, drawn by our "Hancock to Philadelphia" sign. It is here that the Lehigh River, one of the largest of the Delaware's tributaries, flows over a V-shaped dam just before it comes into the Delaware.

Today was the easiest day of the entire trip, and we probably could have stopped at Easton. But once you're on the river, you feel like you just want to keep going. It's okay to stop and fish and swim, but you don't feel like stopping at a city.

It was only a little after 3 p.m. when we approached the bridge at Riegelsville, Pennsylvania. We had covered twenty-two miles in about six hours. Before we landed, we had to pay a special toll—two white ducks looking for food came quacking up to us from shore. Matt tossed them some bread.

You would think all that paddling would make us hungry, but we never ate much during the day. That morning, in Riverton, we had had a breakfast of delicious peanut butter waffles. But other than those, all we had eaten were some chips, fruit, and candy bars.

The Riegelsville Hotel, where we were staying, was really fancy. We had a big supper in the dining room. They made great soup. Matt couldn't finish his huge bowl of spaghetti and meatballs.

After dinner, we walked across the bridge to Riegelsville, New Jersey, to find a phone so that Matt could call his mom and dad and tell them everything was okay. There was a phone in the hotel, but it was crowded and noisy.

There are two Riegelsvilles—one in New Jersey and one across the river in Pennsylvania. We were staying in the Riegelsville Hotel in Pennsylvania.

Over in Riegelsville, New Jersey, Matt and I stopped at a bar and grill so he could call home. They didn't have a phone, but they had a pool table.

"Want to shoot a game of pool?" I asked Matt.

"Sure, but I'm not very good," he answered.

Matt wasn't that bad and with a little practice he'd win his share of games. But I hate to lose, and I didn't. We shot another game and had a soda. One of the local guys challenged me. This time I lost.

Back at the hotel, with things a little more quiet, Matt finally called. It was late, and day seven was over. Tomorrow we would face our first wing dam.

CHAPTER 8

A Day with Kayakers, Then a Surprise - From Riegelsville to Lambertville

We slid through the morning haze down the steep bank in front of the Riegelsville Hotel to our canoe. I think I could have slept another three hours, and I know Matt could have, but we were getting anxious to finish the trip.

We had stored our canoe, our tent, clothes, paddles, and food in some bushes underneath the bridge the night before. When we turned the canoe over to put it into the water, we saw that somehow we had broken the back seat where I sat. It wasn't all the way busted, but I had to stuff the waterproof sack my clothes were in underneath the broken seat to keep it up.

We planned to spend the night camping at Bull's Island, about twenty miles downriver. There was a public campground on the New Jersey side of the river. Just before Bull's Island, at Lumberville, we would hit our first wing dam.

The Delaware has three wing dams: at Lumberville, Lambertville, and Scudders Falls. The wing dams were built in the 1800s to help the rafters by creating small lakes to store the rafts in until they were ready to go over the rapids. Some creative and courageous local people would charge to guide the rafts through the rapids. In later years, the wing dams were reinforced with concrete to create small reservoirs for drinking water.

The wing dams can be dangerous. If the river is high, and you go over the dam, you can get trapped in the water below the dam. It's like a whirlpool. The

The morning fog lifts slowly over the bridge joining Riegelsville, New Jersey, in the distance, to Riegelsville, Pennsylvania.

rushing water keeps holding you down. Even if you have a life jacket on, there's a good chance you'll drown.

It would be important for us to go through the center chute of the dam. There was a Class I Plus rapid at the chute's center. We weren't too worried about the rapid, but we didn't want to go over the dam.

Near Frenchtown, New Jersey, at the end of Upper Black Eddy, a long and wide stretch of river, we met up with five kayakers.

A kayak is a sleek, shallow boat, usually paddled by one person. It's easy to handle, fast, and, if you know what you're doing, you can flip completely over underwater and come up again.

"Watch, I'll show you," said one of the kayakers.

He zipped past us, stopped, and poked his paddle into the water.

"He's checking to see if there are any rocks or shallow spots," explained his friend. "You have to be careful not to hit your head on the bottom."

Then, with a quick movement to his side and some furious paddling, he was under and up on the other side.

"He's always showing off," kidded another friend.

The kayakers told us we should have no problem with the wing dam at Lumberville as long as we stayed in the middle.

Unfortunately, now we were in big eddies, two to three hundred yards wide, and several jet skis and motor boats raced up and down the middle of the river. Matt loves to go fast, and he loves the power of jet skis and motor boats. But when you're canoeing slow and easy, and most of the trip you haven't seen speed boats and jet skis, they get in the way. Even Matt had to admit that.

Some people along the Delaware are signing petitions asking the government to ban jet skis. Matt said he wasn't sure he agreed with that, and I'm not sure I do either. Still, as one person said, "That's a lot of noise for one man's fun."

Near Frenchtown we meet a few kayakers who make the day more enjoyable for us.

These jet skis and motor boats kept us pinned to the New Jersey side of the river, where the maps said the current was. Matt thought the maps were wrong, because it looked to him as if the current was on the Pennsylvania side of the river.

I figured we could hug the shoreline right up to the dam at Lumberville. Once there, we could walk out on it and study the rapid.

Then suddenly we saw it. Or, really, we didn't see it. The river that is. It just dropped out of sight. We both realized what was happening. The water was higher than we had thought it would be, maybe from rain upriver. Whatever the reason, the river was going over the wing dam! And we were heading right for it.

We should have been out in the middle looking for the chute. Instead, we were staying near shore away from the jet skis, and now we were fewer than forty yards from the dam.

"Oh no!" Matt cried out as he raised himself up to see over the dam.

"Cut to the right!" I yelled.

We cut hard and paddled toward the center chute. Now we were sideways to the current, and the river was pushing us towards the dam. There are television shows that capture real-life rescues on video. Often those rescues are of people trapped in rivers. And sometimes, the people who are trapped went over just this kind of a low wing dam. Looking back on it now, I realize that we were very lucky. If we had gone over the dam sideways, there's no telling what could have happened to us.

Ten yards from the dam we shot into the rapid. Right in front of us were the biggest waves we had seen. Bigger than Skinners Falls, bigger than Mongaup, bigger than Foul Rift. They were close to four feet high, and we were headed right into them.

The river grabbed us and jerked us forward.

"Here we go!" Matt cried.

"Keep paddling," I yelled.

My heart pounded furiously as I beat at the waves.

"No more rapids!" Matt yelled back.

"We're gonna make it!" I shouted, though I was sure we were going to be swamped.

We shot up one wave, down the other side of it, and then hurtled into another that raged over our heads. I heard Matt cry out, "Oh no!"

Somehow, and I don't know how, we made it through the center chute without capsizing. We fought our way through the rest of the rapid. Silently, we headed towards shore at Bull's Island, the Lumberville wing dam a bad memory behind us.

At Bull's Island we discovered that the campsites were closed for repairs. It was only about 4 p.m. We weren't thrilled about going on after our near disaster at the wing dam, but we didn't have much choice. I figured we could make it to Lambertville by about 6 p.m., so we kept going.

This had been a long day. Instead of going about twenty miles, we had gone twenty-five miles. We'd had a big

scare at Lumberville, but we had also met some pleasant and memorable people, the kayakers.

We pulled the boat ashore at Lewis Island, right next to Lambertville. The island was owned by Fred Lewis, the last licensed shad netter on the Delaware. I had heard about Fred. He was one of the people I had hoped we would meet.

As we unloaded our gear, Matt and I got into another argument.

"Are you going to help with some of the gear?" I asked Matt, who stood over by the grass lawn near Fred's house.

"I'm helping," he replied.

"Not much," I snapped.

"I'm doing more than you are," he answered.

Ducks swim past our canoe perched on Lewis Island in Lambertville, New Jersey. Across the river sits New Hope, Pennsylvania.

Tourists can take a scenic trip up the river from New Hope.

"You've got to be kidding me. You do next to nothing," I said, looking hard at him.

"Yeah. Well, who made you boss?" Matt said.

Both of us were tired, and neither of us was willing to give an inch right then.

"You're always so serious. And you're always criticizing me. Why don't you ease up?"

"All I want from you is respect and for you to do your fair share of the work," I replied.

"I do," he snapped.

"Not from my point of view, you don't," I shot back.

Matt stared at me for a moment, then turned his head and walked away.

Arguments aren't pleasant, but they're difficult to avoid when you spend eight or ten hours a day together paddling a canoe. It's hard work. Things don't always go the way you want them to. Sometimes you get frustrated and lose your temper.

Matt and I were stuck with each other. So Matt went for a walk to get a break. There wasn't much

either one of us could do. I knew Matt didn't want to quit, and neither did I. We really couldn't anyway. So the best thing to do was to get away from each other for a while.

Later that night, after dinner, we sat on the porch of Fred Lewis's house near the river. We watched hundreds of fireflies light up his yard, and we talked with him about shad netting. Fred Lewis is not like most people you meet. He's been netting shad on the Delaware most of his life. He's seventy-seven, and he started netting when he was fifteen. His father first netted shad way back in 1888. When he speaks about the Delaware River, the river is not a thing. It's his tradition, his family, his existence.

The way you net shad is to pull a big net out fifty yards or more into the river when the shad swim upriver to spawn in spring. They swim together in large schools, so by dragging the net up the river and pulling it across river and then down the river and back to shore, you sometimes catch a few hundred shad at a time.

Every spring, at the same time that the shad start to run upriver to spawn, the popcornlike buds of the shad bushes bloom in the Upper and Middle Delaware.

Besides shad, Fred has caught forty-seven different kinds of fish, including a four-foot-long muskellunge and an eleven-pound catfish.

Pollution in the Delaware once

stopped the shad from coming upriver to spawn. In the 1940s the pollution was so bad that pilots flying over Philadelphia were warned not to worry about the smell below—it was only the river.

Thanks to the efforts of many people, the Delaware is a remarkably clean river today. From Hancock even to the northern edges of the huge city of Philadelphia, eagles, blue herons, ducks, beavers, otters, muskrats, trout, bass, pike, eel, shad, and other animals and fish are coming back and surviving.

Fred Lewis is one of the people who helped clean up the river, and he did it by watching what the shad do.

Shad are anadromous, which means they live in the ocean and then spawn in fresh water. Early each spring the adults swim from the Atlantic Ocean up rivers like the Delaware. As we canoed downriver, we saw thousands of "spent" shad that had died naturally after they had spawned.

"Shad are a good barometer of water quality," Fred told us.

By the early 1940s, the shad had stopped running up the Delaware. Then, there were five shad netters on the river. Today, there is only one—Fred Lewis.

"My dad kept his equipment up," said Fred. "He said that if they cleaned up the pollution, the shad would be back."

Biologists found that the shad would come only to Philadelphia and would go no further. There they hit a two-mile-long stretch of polluted water. The female shad would drop their eggs in the warm water; the males would fertilize them, but the eggs needed the clean water of the Upper Delaware to incubate. Only a few shad were born in the polluted water.

Armed with the facts about the shad and other animals, the federal government pressured Philadelphia and Camden, New Jersey, to clean up the water. The cities complied, starting a massive clean-up effort.

Today, the shad population is back. Fred Lewis estimated that 500,000 shad ran upriver this spring. That means that the pollution has been drastically reduced.

I watched Matt as he listened closely to Fred Lewis, the way I've seen him listen to his grandfather talk about fishing. Fred had knowledge of the river that few people have, and Matt respected that. Matt wanted to learn as much as he could from Fred in that short time, and he peppered him with questions. Fred never tired of answering. I could have stayed and talked and watched all night, but the river had tired us out. And tomorrow morning we had to face the biggest rapid of the whole trip—Wells Falls at the Lambertville wing dam.

Matt talks with Fred Lewis, seventy-seven, the only licensed shad netter left on the Delaware River.

I got up early this morning and let Matt sleep. I found a path through the woods to the wing dam and walked out to look at Wells Falls. About a dozen turkey buzzards flew off the dam as I approached. They reminded me of day three. Since buzzards feast on dead animals, I didn't take their presence as a good sign.

However, I saw that we would be able to paddle right up to the wing dam, walk out on it, and then decide what to do. I went back and woke up Matt.

After we broke camp, we walked across the bridge to meet the mayor of New Hope, James Magill. Jim, who is eighty, knows the history of his Pennsylvania town. He took us around and patiently showed us a lot of the old buildings in town. Originally named Wells Ferry, New Hope got its present name in 1790, when a fire destroyed the mills of Benjamin Parry. Parry liked to look at the bright side of things, so when he rebuilt the mills, he called the town New Hope Mills.

In the late 1800s, the beauty of the Delaware River attracted artists to the area, and New Hope became a center for art. Ever since then, artists, writers, shopkeepers, sculptors, actors, and thousands of tourists flock to New Hope.

"New Hope is synonymous with art," said Mayor Magill. "Today, our biggest problem is parking.

Before we headed south on day nine, we talked with Jim Magill, eighty, the mayor of New Hope, Pennsylvania. Matt and Mayor Magill take a look at the Parry Mansion in the center of New Hope.

We're a tourist town fast running out of parking space."

We saw some of the cars that park in New Hope—Corvettes, Jaguars, Porsches, BMWs, and even an Alfa Romeo.

Around 11 a.m. we put our simple, paddle-powered canoe in the water and crept along the New Jersey shoreline to the Lambertville wing dam and the Wells Falls rapids. We walked out on the dam to the middle of the river. These were the biggest rapids of the river—Class II Plus followed by a Class II. Not only did they have big waves, three feet and higher, but there were huge boulders and rock ledges right in the middle that we had to maneuver around.

We studied the rapids for about twenty minutes, and then we decided to go around the Class II Plus and

Wells Falls, just past the Lambertville wing dam, is one of the most for-midable rapids on the river.

At Washington Crossing, Matt stands at the entrance to McConkey's Ferry Inn, the only building that stood when George Washington and his men crossed the Delaware for their surprise attack on the British at Trenton, New Jersey.

put into the river just above the Class II rapids. We lifted the canoe over the wing dam into a little backwater riffle, bypassed the Class II Plus, and entered the main current at the start of the Class II.

We took in some water going through the Class II, but nothing too bad.

About seven miles south of New Hope we stopped at Washington Crossing, where George Washington crossed the Delaware to spring a surprise attack on the Hessian soldiers during the Revolution. I think what impressed us the most were the boats Washington used to cross the river on Christmas Day in 1776. They're called Durham boats. They're big but have no seats. I could just imagine all these guys scrunched up in them, crossing the river in winter, wondering what they'd find when they got to the other side, wondering if they'd win the battle, or be captured or killed.

We talked to a few kids who lived nearby and were visiting Washington Crossing.

"Being a revolutionary soldier looks real hard," said John Shedden, a twelve-year-old. "They had to wrap cloths around their feet. I don't know if I could do it. We just pop food in a microwave, but they had to make fires and all."

"It was probably pretty tough," Sara Kilroy, also twelve, agreed. "Washington was a very brave man. They were losing all these battles. They could have given up, but they didn't. They kept going."

Washington didn't give up. He had lost several battles on Long Island, and in New York City and New Jersey. He then crossed the Delaware into Pennsylvania. When he did, he took with him those Durham boats, which were used to carry coal. On Christmas Day he used those same boats to carry eighteen cannon and about twenty-four hundred men back across the river to New Jersey.

Washington needed a victory badly. He actually got three in ten days. First, he captured nine hundred Hessian soldiers at Trenton. On January 2, in the Second Battle of Trenton, he beat the Hessians again. A few days later, in the Battle of Princeton, he beat the British army.

Historians still marvel at what Washington and his Continental Army did by crossing the Delaware. It was a very risky move that could have meant the end of the Revolution if Washington had lost. But his personal courage and that of his men brought victory and, soon after, freedom for the colonies.

Once a year, on Christmas Day, area residents re-enact that historic crossing of the Delaware.

Washington Crossing was an interesting place,

Trenton, the capital of New Jersey, lies ahead of us.

but we had to keep going if we were to reach Trenton before dark. Trenton was only eight miles downriver, but we still had one more wing dam to go through.

Scudders Falls was a Class I Plus rapid, and the wing dam there turned out to be two rock and cement walls that extended from the edge of the river toward the middle. It was easy to get through, and toward the end of the rapid we both jumped in the water and floated for a while just hanging onto the canoe. That was so relaxing, another of those dreamlike moments when time stops. We would have stayed there the rest of the day, if we hadn't had important business ahead of us.

About two miles away from Trenton we could see the tall buildings of a big city. And just offshore, on the New Jersey side, we saw a beaver. By the time we got out of the river we would be in tidewater, where water from the Delaware Bay flowed upriver. We had one last rapid to go through—Trenton Falls.

Our map showed Trenton Falls as a Class I Minus followed by a Class I—easy. But the book also said that if the tide was out, Trenton Falls could be a dangerous Class II rapid. We hit it at low tide. This was the closest we came to tipping over.

It was a maze of rock ledges that went on for about a mile. What looked like chutes turned out to have rocks hidden underneath. At one point we hit a hidden rock head on. The back of the canoe spun around and hit another rock. When it did, Matt went flying out of the canoe into a shallow pool beyond the ledge. He came up sputtering and cursing but immediately grabbed the canoe and stopped it from turning over. Then he climbed onto a ledge and stepped back into the canoe.

That night we stored the canoe at Jack's Marina, a huge speedboat marina in south Trenton. It was longer than a football field, and the boats were stacked three high. Our little canoe looked puny next to the big cabin cruisers and speedboats. We put our gear inside the marina and took a taxi to a motel.

Tomorrow, the trip would be over.

Matt sits near the Delaware Canal that runs from Bristol, Pennsylvania, to Easton, Pennsylvania.

Several weeks before our trip, I had driven the length of the river to Philadelphia and met some members of the Coast Guard Auxiliary, volunteers who help boaters when they get into trouble. They told me what to expect from Trenton to Philadelphia. I had also notified the Coast Guard and the New Jersey State Police about our plans. I figured it was about sixteen miles from Trenton to Neshaminy State Park, just north of Philadelphia.

The night before we had paddled under Trenton's famous sign—"Trenton Makes and the World Takes." The sign is a reminder of the key role Trenton played during the Industrial Revolution in our country. Trenton, New Jersey's state capital, was founded in 1721 by businessman William Trent. At the end of the Revolution, Trenton and Princeton, New Jersey, each served for a time as the nation's capital. Trenton almost became the permanent federal capital in 1784, but George Washington squelched the idea. It became New Jersey's capital in 1790.

We were supposed to meet with the governor of New Jersey, Jim Florio, while we were in Trenton, but he was away at the Democratic National Convention. I told Matt that we were far more important than the Democratic Convention and certainly better publicity. Governor Florio sent a letter congratulating us.

Down here the river is more than a half mile

If we had had time and energy, we might have stopped to visit the Pennsbury Mansion, the historic home of William Penn.

wide. It's no longer different shades of brown, black, and green, but grayish blue from the blend of ocean water in it. When we left Hancock, in the cold and rain ten days earlier, the water temperature was probably about 66 degrees. Down here, the tidal waters felt like bath water.

Matt and I were both excited about the trip being over. We figured we could paddle the last sixteen miles in no time. We were wrong. Really wrong. We didn't realize how brutal paddling in tidal water can be to inexperienced canoeists.

We left the marina about 11 a.m. It was very hot already. The temperature hit 95 degrees that day.

I had checked the tide, and our timing couldn't have been worse. The tide was coming in for most of

Tired but satisfied, we pull our canoe ashore at Neshaminy State Park, a few miles north of Philadelphia.

The river spreads to more than a half mile in width near Bristol, Pennsylvania, and Burlington, New Jersey.

the time that we were on the river. It wouldn't change until midafternoon. With the water wide and deep, the head wind would be about ten miles an hour, with gusts a lot stronger. And for most of the time the tide would be against us.

We made good time at the start. But the farther we went, the bigger the waves, the hotter the sun, and the stronger the wind. To make matters worse, every ten or fifteen minutes big speedboats and barges would pass us. Every time one went by, we had to turn the canoe into the wake from the boat; otherwise the waves would swamp us.

It was a good thing I had called the Coast Guard Auxiliary before we left. About noon, two of their members in a cabin cruiser started to follow us just to make sure we didn't get into any trouble.

We canoed past a huge boat dock, then past a big garbage landfill. A little later, we canoed past Pennsbury Mansion. Built in the 1680s, this was William Penn's home in the land of his "Holy Experiment" of religious tolerance and brotherly love.

After Penn's death, his stately mansion and its surrounding buildings literally collapsed and rotted.

But through the efforts of Pennsylvania state officials and the Pennsylvania Historical and Museum Commission, Pennsbury Mansion is now rebuilt and run as a museum by the commission and the Pennsbury Society.

Further on, we stopped for a break in the shade of some willow trees. The sun-drenched water was bathtub warm. Boy, did I want to stay there all day. The rest didn't help. The heat, the big waves, the wind — they were all wearing us down. By 1:30 p.m., Matt was exhausted, and I was fading fast. He couldn't paddle any more, and I didn't know how long I could keep going. We got into another argument. It was mostly me yelling at Matt, telling him to paddle. But I could see that he was exhausted.

We both just wanted the trip to be over. We had thought today would be easy. It was turning into the hardest day of the trip.

By now, I was the only one paddling. We weren't making good time at all. The river was getting wider, and the waves bigger. When I had driven down to this section before our trip, the river didn't look that big. But now, sitting in a canoe in the middle of it, the river looked huge. We felt small and vulnerable.

Around 3 p.m., we pulled alongside the Coast Guard Auxiliary boat. Mike Ryan and Carol Frankowicz, two volunteers, gave us some water and told us that we still had six miles to go. They started to tow us for a little while. I watched Matt, and I could tell that he was beat. And frankly, so was I.

"Do you want us to tow you the rest of the way?" asked Carol.

"What do you think?" I asked Matt.

He shrugged his shoulders. "I don't care," he answered.

It bugged me to have to end our trip being towed, but I didn't think we could make it otherwise.

"Keep towing us," I said.

We were both relieved.

But here's the strangest part. Even though we were being towed, the last six miles turned out to be the hardest, by far, of the entire trip. The waves from the river and the wake from the front of Mike's boat were nearly swamping us. We were getting soaked from every boat that went by. The water was just pouring into our canoe.

Matt was holding onto the tow rope, and Carol was pulling up on it each time a wave from Mike's boat hit us. We couldn't tie the rope onto the canoe, because it would be too difficult to control the canoe each time the wake from the boat slammed into us. It was like going through six miles of Class II Plus rapids. We hadn't seen anything like it for the entire trip.

At one point, I looked down and saw that I was sitting in eight inches of water and didn't even realize it.

"Start bailing," Matt yelled at me.

And we started bailing.

I didn't think we were going to make it. I thought for sure that the canoe would be swamped less than a mile from the end.

It was about 5 p.m. when we landed at Neshaminy State Park. Both of us were weak and nauseous. Matt's hands were so sore from holding on the rope that he could barely open them up, and our backs were stiff and ached. The canoe was still filled with several inches of water.

But the trip was over.

There were a couple of newspaper reporters and photographers waiting for us. A few kids swimming and some people putting in jet skis looked at us as if we were weird. I suppose we did look strange, two dirty-looking guys in a beat-up aluminum canoe filled with water being towed to shore by a cabin cruiser.

No bands played for us. No congratulations from anybody, except the newspaper people. I don't know what we expected, but it really didn't matter. We had finished what we had set out to do. That was all we wanted.

Even the fact that we had to be towed didn't really bother us. It was an unforeseen finish. I guess it kind of showed our weakness, and our foolishness at not being prepared for the big water. Matt's father had said the river would teach us something. Sometimes you learn what you did wrong.

We had traveled 215 miles in ten days. That's about 150,000 times of sticking a paddle into the water, pulling it back, and then lifting it out of the water.

We started out as newcomers to canoeing. At the end, I wouldn't say we were experts, but we had gone through nine Class II rapids and we didn't tip over once. We were both very proud of that.

Matt and I were satisfied with what we had done, but we were ready to go home.

My daughter, Julia, watches as I unload our gear.

EPILOGUE

As far as we know, Matt Smith is one of the youngest persons, if not the youngest, in this century to canoe from the start of the Delaware to Philadelphia.

Huge barges ply the waters of the Delaware River where the Schuylkill River enters it in Philadelphia.

People ask me, "Did you have fun?" They don't understand. Paddling sometimes eight or ten hours a day isn't fun. There were some things that were fun, and there are some places that I'd like to go back to. But canoeing 215 miles isn't fun.

I'm glad I did it. I feel like I accomplished something. But I don't plan on doing it again.

As I said at the beginning, my father said the river would teach me something. It did. I learned some things about myself. I've done something only a few people have ever done. I canoed the Delaware from Hancock to Philadelphia. And I might even be the youngest person to ever do it, at least in modern times.

When I got home, I played some basketball to get my legs back into shape and rode my motor bike, just to feel the power of going somewhere without using my own strength.

I've got a lot of time to think about the cuts, bruises, and bug bites, and when I lie down, I can feel my bones settle back into place.

Looking back on the trip, I think you have to really want to do something to do it. You can't just keep putting things off until your life is gone.

You just have to go out and do them.

Matthew Smith

YOU MIGHT LIKE TO KNOW...

How the Delaware Quenches New York City's Thirst

Pepacton Reservoir

Surrounded by farm land, the East and West branches of the Delaware begin as small swamps in the rolling hills of the Catskill Mountains. In the early 1900s, New York City officials saw that the city's increasing population and growing industries would need millions of gallons of water. First, the city dammed the waters in Westchester County, about twenty miles north of the city. But New York needed much more water. By the 1930s, the city began plans to dam both the East and West branches of the Delaware. Today, two huge reservoirs—the Cannonsville on the West Branch and the Pepacton on the East Branch—are part of a complex storage system that supplies water to millions of people in the city.

The state and federal governments decided that the city's need for drinking water was more important than the needs of the farmers in upstate New York. The state granted the city the right of "condemnation," which means that the city has the right to take farm property as long as it pays owners a fair-market price for their land. New York City recently announced that it will buy more property around the reservoirs to protect the quality of its drinking water.

Providing water for the city has long been a problem. Reservoirs have solved that for the time being, but not everybody was happy when New York City built these reservoirs. Some people had to move because the reservoirs destroyed their homes. Whole villages were flooded when the rivers were dammed.

Some property owners near the reservoirs resent having to sell. Others don't mind. The city also pays taxes on the land that it buys, which means that taxes on property near the reservoirs are low.

The argument between the city and upstate farmers is complicated and not easily solved. Both sides have valid points. The city's demand for clean drinking water is just one of many battles about the Delaware River.

Fighting for Water Rights

East and West meet

In Hancock, where the East and West branches of the Delaware meet, the Delaware begins its 330-mile journey to the Delaware Bay. The Delaware isn't one of our country's longest rivers, but because of all of the people who use its waters, it is one of the most sought-after watersheds in the world.

A watershed is all the land that drains its water either above ground or underground into one river. More than 20 million people, including the residents of New York City, Philadelphia, Trenton, and Camden, use the water of the 12,755 square miles of the Delaware River watershed.

The Lenni Lenape (le nah' pay), the native Americans who lived and hunted along the banks of the Delaware River for centuries, rarely, if ever, fought over using the water of the Delaware. The white men and women who followed Henry Hudson after he found the river in 1609, however, began to squabble about water rights almost from the start. The Delaware, named for the colonial governor of Virginia, Lord De La Warr, today forms part of the boundary between the states of Pennsylvania and New Jersey, New Jersey and Delaware, and Pennsylvania and New York. Today, those states and their large cities argue about who controls the river.

Twice—in 1931 and in 1954—the Supreme Court had to tell the states and cities who could do what with the river. Both times, New York City said it needed more drinking water from the Delaware. The states said no. So the court told the city how much water it could take from the Delaware River. Today, the city takes no more than 800 million gallons of water a day. Each reservoir has a huge pipe that runs underground to New York City. And the water is pumped from the reservoirs to the city. The court also determined that no less than 1,750 cubic feet per second must flow downriver. This protects the fragile ecosystem in the river. The court appointed a river master to make sure that the city doesn't take too much water.

Zane Grey, the Master of the Western

Zane Grey Museum

Zane Grey wrote eighty-nine books, most of them westerns. More than one hundred movies were made from his stories. Before Zane Grey died in 1939, he earned more than $37 million.

He started out as a dentist, and rumor has it that Doc Holliday, a dentist turned gunfighter, may have attended the same school as Grey. For several years, Zane Grey and his wife, Dolly, lived in a big white house near where the Lackawaxen River flows into the Delaware. Zane Grey and Dolly moved to California to make movies. But when they died, their ashes were buried in the cemetery near the house that they loved. Today, the National Park Service has restored their home and made it a museum.

About a Bridge-Building Genius

We take bridges for granted. Whether we're crossing the George Washington Bridge in New York City, the Golden Gate Bridge in San Francisco, or a simple country bridge such as the Roebling Bridge in Lackawaxen, Pennsylvania, we feel pretty sure that the bridge is going to hold up.

In 1848, however, when John Augustus Roebling saw the completion of his first suspension bridge, people came from miles away to see it fall.

The Roebling Bridge was actually a wooden-sided aqueduct filled with water that carried coal barges across the Delaware from Pennsylvania to New York. The bridge was part of the Delaware and Hudson Canal. Before the Roebling Bridge was built, coal shippers crossing the river and log rafters coming down the river would often collide on the river near Lackawaxen and fight for who was going to go first.

Roebling had an answer to that problem: build an aqueduct bridge over the river. The day the bridge opened folks came lined up to see the first coal barge cross the Delaware in Roebling's bridge suspended above the river. The people figured the weight of the barge would force the bridge to collapse.

The bridge didn't collapse. For more than fifty years, barges crossed the Delaware River in Roebling's suspension bridge, the oldest in the United States. By the early 1900s, the barge business had faded, and the aqueduct bridge was converted for horses and then cars. Today, Roebling Bridge has been restored with the help of the National Park Service, and it still carries cars.

John Augustus Roebling went on to build other suspension bridges, including the famous Brooklyn Bridge.

About the Battle to Save the River

The Water Gap

The Delaware River is one of the most picturesque rivers in the United States, but the place where it starts is only a few hours' drive from one of the world's most populated areas. Not only do metropolitan areas want the Delaware's water for drinking, but since the early 1960s, millions of fishermen, canoeists, swimmers, and boaters have visited the Middle and Upper Delaware. Officials estimate that two hundred thousand people come to the Upper Delaware each year.

The pressure to preserve this incredible river has been increasing in recent years. While most people agree that the river must be protected, not everyone agrees how.

In 1978 the federal government said that the Upper Delaware River was a special national treasure that needed to be protected from pollution and overdevelopment. The government set aside seventy-three miles of the Delaware, from Hancock to Port Jervis, as part of the National Wild and Scenic River System.

But unlike other national parks, the federal government didn't buy all of the land along the Upper Delaware. Instead, it said private land owners could keep their property, but it also set rules for protecting the river. The National Park Service, the states of New York and Pennsylvania, and local representatives now determine how to best protect the river.

Not everyone in the river valley wants the Park Service around. That may be hard for people who don't live along the Delaware River to understand. Some of the people who have lived in the river valley for generations are fiercely independent, and they distrust any government involvement. They believe they can care for the river better than any federal agency because the river valley is their home.

There are great differences in opinion about how best to care for the river, but the Delaware is now protected by the federal government. The government has said that what happens in the Delaware River and along its shores is important not only to the people who live in the river valley but to the nation, too. It would literally take an act of Congress to change that.

Some people still fear the National Park Service. They believe that the federal government will take their land or restrict their business. Others say that the Upper Delaware is a better place because of the Park Service. They point out that not only has the Park Service restored historic buildings, but drownings in the river have decreased since the Park Service Rangers arrived.

A Place to Argue

It would have been easier for the government to buy all of the land in the Upper Delaware. It also would have cost millions of dollars to do so. Instead, for the first time in the history of our country, the federal government decided to become partners with local residents to help protect a natural resource. Being a partner instead of the property manager is a new role for the federal government, and it doesn't come easy.

Part of the new government plan was to form the Upper Delaware Council, made up of local, state, and federal representatives who work with the National Park Service to see that federal regulations are followed. When you get so many different people together, it's hard to always agree. The members of the council and the public often argue about jet skis, pollution control, zoning laws, safety, law enforcement, and a host of other issues. The job of the council is to make sure the Upper Delaware River is protected, without over-regulating the lives of river residents.

Take a Look at a River Town

The Delaware makes a ninety-degree turn to the south and becomes a lot wider at the City of Port Jervis, New York, named for John B. Jervis, the chief engineer of the Delaware and Hudson Canal. Built in 1828, the canal connected Honesdale, Pennsylvania, with Rondout, New York, on the Hudson River. Port Jervis is about halfway between the two towns.

For decades, rafters, canal men and women, and railroaders found rest and plenty of fun in Port Jervis. Like many towns and villages along the river, Port Jervis always faces the threat of floods. Even today, early spring rains and melting ice can spell disaster for towns such as Port Jervis.

Most of the Upper Delaware freezes in a cold winter. When a thaw comes in late January, February, or even March, the ice cracks and booms and breaks up into huge ice cakes several feet thick and dozens of feet long and wide. When the ice cakes head downriver, people call it an "ice out."

In 1981, after a bitterly cold winter, the Delaware River's ice broke loose and got hung up south of the U.S. Route 84 Bridge in Port Jervis. The river rose more than fourteen feet in less than an hour, flooding all of downtown Port Jervis and backing up streams that flooded villages almost as far north as Hancock.

A Vengence Seeker and a Conservationist

A lot of interesting people settled along the Delaware. Some were good; some weren't. The village of Milford, Pennsylvania, just south of Port Jervis, produced two well-known men—Tom Quick and Gifford Pinchot.

Tom Quick is remembered for his hatred of native Americans. He and his family were once friendly with the Lenni Lenape who lived in the area. But after the outbreak of the French and Indian War, Tom's father was ambushed and killed by Indians. Tom watched helplessly from the woods as they scalped his wounded father and celebrated his death. Tom Quick then began a one-man war to kill as many Indians as he could.

By the time of his death Quick had reportedly killed ninety-nine native Americans. Legend has it that when news of Tom Quick's death reached the Lenape, some of the warriors dug up his body, cut it up, and sent the pieces to villages as proof of Tom Quick's death. Some people believe—though it's never been proven—that Tom Quick died from smallpox. If true, Tom Quick was far more lethal dead than alive.

Gifford Pinchot, on the other hand, is remembered for his extraordinary efforts in saving America's forests. He served as chief of the Forest Service under President Theodore Roosevelt and was twice elected governor of Pennsylvania. Pinchot is considered the father of forestry management in the United States. You can visit Pinchot's home, a mammoth forty-one-room mansion called Grey Towers near Milford.

More about the Delaware and Raritan Canal

At Bull's Island the Delaware and Raritan Canal begins. An incredible engineering feat, the canal was completed in 1834 and was built out of stone, mostly by Irish immigrants. It is seventy-five feet wide, eight feet deep, and sixty-six miles long. The engineers took water from the Delaware and redirected it through the canal south to Trenton. This water fills the canal that connects the Delaware River with the Raritan River in eastern New Jersey. The canal is still important today. It carries drinking water to communities throughout New Jersey. Much of it is a park used by walkers, joggers, and bicyclists.

INDEX

Appalachian Mountains, 24
Appalachian Trail, 24, 27
Atlantic Ocean, 7, 16, 35, 44

Basket Brook, 9
bass, 25, 35
Battle of Princeton, 38
beavers, 35, 39
Belvidere, N.J., 21, 27, 28
Big Cedar Rift, 16
Brandt, Chief Joseph, 16
Brooklyn Bridge, 15, 46
Bull's Island, 31, 33, 47
Butlers Falls, 19

Callicoon, N.Y., 8, 10, 11, 13
Callicoon Bridge, 10
Camden, N.J., 36, 46
canals, 11-12, 28, 47
Cannonsville Reservoir, 45
Canoeing the Delaware River, 28
Capush Rift, 29, 30
Catfish, 34
Catskill Mountains, 45
Cheripko, Julia, 13, 20, 43; Valray, 10,
    13, 20
Christenberry, Mike, 21
coal, 28, 46
Coast Guard, 41; Auxiliary, 41, 42
Colang Creek, 15
Colang Rift, 15

dams, 24-25, 45. *See also* drinking water,
    wing dams
De La Warr, Lord, 45
Delaware (state), 45
Delaware and Hudson Canal, 47
Delaware and Raritan Canal, 28, 47
Delaware Bay, 39, 47
Delaware Canal, 30
Delaware River Basin Commission, 10, 47
Delaware River Joint Toll Bridge
    Commission, 28
Delaware River watershed, 45
Delaware Water Gap, 27, 28; National
    Recreational Area, 24
Dingman, Andrew, 21
Dingmans Ferry, Pa., 21, 23
drinking water, 25, 31, 45, 46, 47
drownings, 12, 46
ducks, 8, 24, 30, 33, 35
Dunkirk, N.Y., 13
Durham boats, 38

eagles, 10, 35
East Branch, 7, 8, 25, 45
East Stroudsburg, Pa., 27
Easton, Pa., 30
eddies, 9, 32
eel weirs, 10, 16, 17, 19

eels, 16, 35
Equinunk, Pa., 8

Field & Stream, 15
fishing, 8, 21, 25, 34
floods, 47
Florio, (Governor) Jim, 41
Foul Rift, 21, 28, 29, 33
Frankowicz, Carol, 42-43
Frenchtown, N.J., 32

Great New York and Erie Railway, 13
Grey, Dolly, 46
Grey, Zane, 15-16, 46; museum, 15-16, 46
Grey Towers, 47

Hancock, N.Y., 8, 10, 34, 41, 44, 45, 46, 47
Hankins, N.Y., 10
Hawks' Nest, 14, 20; Restaurant, 20
herons, 8, 24, 35
High Point, N.J., 20
Hoboken, N.J., 13
Honesdale, Pa., 47
Hudson, Henry, 45
Hudson River, 47
Hughes, Teg, 28, 29
Hurryback River House, 27-28

industrial revolution, 41
inns, 28
Interstate Route 80, 27

Jack's Marina (Trenton), 39
Jervis, John B., 47
jet skis, 32, 47

Karcher, James, 21
kayaks, 31, 32, 33
Kean, Paul, 17, 19
Kean's landing, 17
Kilroy, Sara, 38
Kittatinny Mountains, 24

Lackawaxen, Pa., 11, 15
Lackawaxen River, 46
Lambertville, N.J., 31, 33, 37.
    See also wing dams
Lehigh River, 30
Lenni Lenape, 19, 20, 45, 47
Letcher, Gary, 28
Lewis, Fred, 33, 34, 35
Lewis Island, 33
Long Eddy, N.Y., 8-9
Long Island, N.Y., 38
Lordville, N.Y., 8
Lumberville, N.J., 31, 33. *See also* wing
    dams

Magill, James, 37
maps, 2, 10, 28, 29, 32

Metropolitan Edison Electric Generating
    Plant, 27
Milford, Pa., 47
Mitchell, Deacon, 11
Mongaup Falls, 10, 19, 33
Mongaup River, 19, 22
muskellunge, 21, 34
muskrats, 35

Narrow Falls Rift, 15
Narrowsburg, N.Y., 13
National Park Service, 15, 24, 46, 47
National Wild and Scenic River System, 46
Neshaminy State Park, 7, 41, 43
Neversink River, 21
New Hope, Pa., 34, 37
New Jersey, 21, 24, 26, 27, 38, 41, 45
New Jersey State Police, 41
New York City, 38, 45; reservoir, 45
New York State, 13, 21, 45, 46, 47

Old Mine Road, 24
otters, 25

paddles, 7
paddling, 23, 41-42
Parry, Benjamin, 37
Penn, William, 42
Pennsbury Mansion, 42
Pennsbury Society, 42
Pennsylvania, 13, 15, 21, 24, 38, 45, 46,
    47
Pennsylvania Historical and Museum
    Commission, 42
Pepacton Reservoir, 45
Philadelphia, 7, 11, 35, 41, 44, 45
pike, 35
Pinchot, Gifford, 47
Point Mountain, 7
pollution (in the Delaware), 13, 28, 35, 47
Pond Eddy, 15, 17, 19
Port Jervis, N.Y., 20, 21, 26, 46, 47
portaging, 21
Portland, Pa., 27
Pratt, Stan, 12
Prentiss, Jerry and Arlene, 28
Princeton, N.J., 41

Quick, Tom, 47

rafting, 11-12, 27, 31, 46, 47
railroads. *See* trains
rapids, 7, 8, 9, 10, 11, 12, 13, 15, 16, 17,
    19, 21, 28, 29, 30, 31, 32, 33, 35, 37,
    38, 39
Raritan River, 47
reservoirs, 45. *See also* dams, drinking
    water
Revolutionary War, 16, 38
Riders of the Purple Sage, 15

Riegelsville, N.J., 29, 30, 31
Riegelsville, Pa., 30
Riegelsville Hotel, 30, 31
Riverton, Pa., 27, 29, 32
Roebling, John Augustus, 15, 46
Roebling Bridge, 15, 17, 46
Rondout, N.Y., 47
Roosevelt, Theodore, 47
Route 84 Bridge, 47
Route 97, N.Y., 20
Ryan, Mike, 42-43

Sargasso Sea, 16
Schultz, Ken, 15, 16, 17
Scudders Falls, 31
Second Battle of Trenton, 38
shad, 33, 34, 35
Shawnee Resort Hotel, 24
Shedden, John, 38
Shohola Rift, 16
Skinner, Daniel, 11
Skinners Falls, 11, 12, 13, 28, 33
Smith, David, 13, 15, 16; James
    (Matthew's father), 5, 7, 13, 15, 16, 20,
    43, 44; James Patrick, 13; Patty, 13;
    Peter, 13, 15, 16
Speers, Sandy, 15, 16, 17
Stairway Rift, 19
swans, mute, 9

Ten Mile River, 11, 15
tidal waters, 41-42
Tocks Island, 24; dam, 24-25
trains, 13, 28, 47
Trent, William, 41
Trenton, N.J., 10, 11, 37, 38, 39, 45, 47
Trenton Falls, 39
trout, 8, 35

Upper Black Eddy, 31
Upper Delaware Council, 47

Wallpack Bend, 23, 24
Washington, George, 38, 41
Washington Crossing, Pa., 38
water rights, 45. *See also* dams, drinking
    water
Wells Falls, 35, 37
Wells Ferry, Pa. *See* New Hope, Pa.
West Branch, 7, 8, 25, 45
Westchester County, 45
wing dams, 21, 24, 30, 31; Lambertville,
    31, 35, 37; Lumberville, 31, 32, 33;
    Scudders Falls, 31, 39; Trenton Falls, 39
Worthington State Forest and Park, 23,
    24, 27

Yulan, N.Y., 13